W9-BON-794

NO EGG
ON YOUR FACE!

Easy and Delicious Egg-Free Recipes
for Kids With Allergies

by **KATRINA JORGENSEN**

CONSULTANT
Amy Durkan MS, RDN, CDN
Nutrition Research Manager
Mount Sinai Medical Center
New York, NY

CAPSTONE PRESS
a capstone imprint

Edge Books are published by Capstone Press,
1710 Roe Crest Drive, North Mankato, Minnesota 56003
www.mycapstone.com

Library of Congress Cataloging-in-Publication Data
Cataloging-in-Publication data is on file with the Library of Congress.
ISBN 978-1-4914-8055-7 (library binding)
ISBN 978-1-4914-8060-1 (eBook PDF)

Editorial Credits
Anna Butzer, editor; Heidi Thompson, designer; Morgan Walters, media researcher;
Sarah Schuette, food stylist; Kathy McColley, production specialist

Design Elements
Shutterstock: avian, design element, Katerina Kirilova, design element, Lena Pan, design
element, Marco Govel, design element, mexrix, design element, Sabina Pittak, design
element, STILLFX, design element, swatchandsoda, design element

Photography by Capstone Studio: Karon Dubke

Editor's note:
Capstone cannot ensure that any food is allergen-free. The only way to be sure a food is
safe is to read all labels carefully, every time. Cross-contamination is also a risk for those
with food allergies. Please call food companies to make sure their manufacturing processes
avoid cross-contamination. Also, always be sure to clean hands, surfaces, and tools
before cooking.

Printed and bound in the USA.
009675F16

TABLE OF CONTENTS

WHAT IS A FOOD ALLERGY?

Our bodies are armed with immune systems. It's the immune system's job to fight infections, viruses, and invaders. Sometimes the immune system identifies a certain food as one of these invaders and attacks it. While our immune system fights, a chemical response is triggered and causes an allergic reaction. Reactions vary greatly from a mild skin irritation to having trouble breathing. Any time you feel you are having a reaction, tell an adult immediately.

The best way to avoid having an allergic reaction is to be aware of what you are eating. Be careful not to consume the allergen that affects you. If you are not sure if that allergen is in a food, ask an adult or read the ingredient label of the food container before eating. Unfortunately, allergens can sometimes be hard to identify in an ingredient list. Check out http://www.foodallergy.org for a full list of hidden egg terms.

Avoiding food allergens can be hard to manage, especially when they are found in so many of our favorite foods. This cookbook will take you on a culinary journey to explore safe versions of some of the dishes you've had to avoid because of an egg allergy.

Kitchen Safety

A safe kitchen is a fun kitchen! Always start your recipes with clean hands, surfaces, and tools. Wash your hands and any tools you may use in future steps of a recipe, especially when handling raw meat. Make sure you have an adult nearby to help you with any task you don't feel comfortable doing, such as cutting vegetables or carrying hot pans.

Have other food allergies? No problem.
Check out the list at the end of each recipe
for substitutions for other common allergens.
Look out for other cool tips and ideas too!

CONVERSIONS

1/4 teaspoon	1.25 grams or milliliters
1/2 teaspoon	2.5 g or mL
1 teaspoon	5 g or mL
1 tablespoon	15 g or mL
1/4 cup	57 g (dry) or 60 mL (liquid)
1/3 cup	75 g (dry) or 80 mL (liquid)
1/2 cup	114 g (dry) or 125 mL (liquid)
2/3 cup	150 g (dry) or 160 mL (liquid)
3/4 cup	170 g (dry) or 175 mL (liquid)
1 cup	227 g (dry) or 240 mL (liquid)
1 quart	950 mL

Fahrenheit (°F)	Celsius (°C)
325°	160°
350°	180°
375°	190°
400°	200°
425°	220°
450°	230°

THE NO-EGG SCRAMBLE

Eggs are a staple in many breakfast foods. But you can create a unique take on a classic early morning meal by using protein-packed chickpeas. You'll want to scramble to make this delicious breakfast entree!

Prep Time: 5 minutes

Cook Time: 10 minutes

Serves 1

6

Ingredients

⅓ cup chickpea flour

¼ cup water

¼ teaspoon salt

¼ teaspoon paprika

¼ teaspoon garlic powder

1 tablespoon olive oil

Tools

small bowl

measuring cups/spoons

whisk

non-stick skillet

spatula

Allergens Eradicated!

No major food allergens found here.

1. Combine the chickpea flour, water, salt, paprika, and garlic powder in a small bowl. Whisk ingredients until mixed well. Set aside.

2. Add the olive oil to the skillet and put over a burner set to medium heat.

3. Add the flour mixture to the skillet when the olive oil is hot. The oil will appear to ripple a bit when it is ready.

4. Allow to cook for about three minutes, or until the edges begin to bubble.

5. Use a spatula to break up the batter into bite-sized pieces. Continue to cook until the batter is cooked through, approximately another two to three minutes.

6. Remove from heat and serve immediately.

CHEF'S TIP

Include your favorite veggies or toppings such as mushrooms, spinach, peppers, or onions. Add them to the skillet after step 3.

BLUEBERRY BREAD

You don't need eggs to make fluffy, rich bread. Plump and juicy blueberries add a punch of flavor and antioxidants to this freshly baked loaf. Start your day with a sweet blueberry treat!

Prep Time: 15 minutes

Cook Time: 1 hour

Makes 1 loaf

Ingredients

cooking spray

2 cups all-purpose flour

1 teaspoon baking soda

1 teaspoon kosher salt

$\frac{1}{3}$ cup oil, such as olive oil

3 ripe bananas

$\frac{3}{4}$ cup sugar

1 teaspoon vanilla extract

1 cup thawed frozen blueberries

Tools

loaf pan

2 mixing bowls

measuring cups/spoons

wooden spoon

fork

toothpick

Allergen Alert!

If you need to avoid wheat,
use a wheat-free flour blend
instead of all-purpose flour.

1. Preheat oven to 325°F. Coat the loaf pan generously with the cooking spray and set aside.

2. Combine the flour, baking soda, and salt in a mixing bowl. Stir well and set aside.

3. Combine the oil, bananas, sugar, and vanilla extract in a second mixing bowl. Using a fork, mash the bananas and mix until they are mostly smooth.

4. Add the banana mixture into the flour mixture. Stir gently until the wet ingredients fully absorb the flour.

5. Pour in the blueberries and stir a few times.

6. Transfer the batter into the greased loaf pan. Then place the pan in the oven for about 45 to 50 minutes. The bread is done when a toothpick inserted into the center comes out clean.

7. Allow to cool for 10 to 15 minutes before slicing and serving. Store leftovers by covering completely for up to one week.

CHEF'S TIP

Transform your loaf into easy on-the-go snacks by making muffins! Instead of using a loaf pan, fill a muffin tin with paper liners. Scoop the batter into each cup, leaving about one-third of each cup empty at the top. Bake for 30 to 35 minutes.

APPLESAUCE WAFFLES

Crispy on the outside, fluffy on the inside, these waffles allow you to skip the eggs without compromising the delicious taste. Dive into the flavors of fall with these sweetly spiced waffles drizzled with maple syrup!

Prep Time: 10 minutes

Cook Time: 5 minutes

Serves 4

Ingredients

2 cups all-purpose flour

1 tablespoon baking powder

¼ teaspoon kosher salt

¼ cup sugar

¼ teaspoon ground cinnamon

2 cups water

½ cup all-natural applesauce

¼ teaspoon maple extract

¼ cup oil, such as olive oil

cooking spray

maple syrup, for serving

Tools

2 mixing bowls

measuring cups/spoons

wooden spoon

waffle iron

fork

Allergen Alert!

Replace all-purpose flour with a wheat-free flour blend to avoid wheat.

1. Combine the flour, baking powder, salt, sugar, and cinnamon in a mixing bowl. Set aside.

2. Combine the water, applesauce, maple extract, and oil in a second mixing bowl. Stir until well blended.

3. Pour the wet ingredients into the bowl of dry ingredients and mix well.

4. Warm up the waffle iron and spray lightly with cooking spray.

5. Pour a portion of batter into the center of the iron (it should fill three-quarters of the iron) and close the lid. Follow the recommended cook time given by the waffle iron brand, or cook until golden brown.

6. Remove from waffle iron with a fork. Repeat steps 4 and 5 until all the batter is used.

7. Serve hot with maple syrup.

TROPICAL GREEK
YOGURT PARFAIT

Who needs eggs for protein! Jump-start your day with an energy-boosting breakfast. With layers of Greek yogurt and crunchy coconut, this parfait is a protein powerhouse!

Prep Time: 5 minutes

Makes 1 parfait

Ingredients

1 cup plain Greek yogurt

2 teaspoons pure honey

½ teaspoon vanilla extract

½ cup frozen diced mango, thawed

½ cup frozen diced pineapple, thawed

¼ cup toasted coconut

Tools

mixing bowl

measuring cups/spoons

spoon

parfait glass or bowl, for serving

1. Combine the Greek yogurt, honey, and vanilla extract in a mixing bowl. Set aside.

2. Assemble your parfait by spreading one-third of the yogurt at the bottom of a parfait glass or bowl. Add one-third of the mango and pineapple. Repeat layers until finished.

3. Top with toasted coconut and serve immediately.

Allergen Alert!

If you are allergic to dairy, use coconut milk or almond milk yogurt instead of the Greek yogurt.

Coconut is classified as a fruit. But if you have a tree nut allergy, please talk to your doctor before eating it.

CHICKEN NUGGETS
AND AVOCADO DIP

Who doesn't love chicken nuggets? But eggs usually help make the crispy, crunchy nugget coating. Not this time! These crispy bite-sized chicken nuggets and the creamy avocado dip are sure to please your entire family.

Prep Time: 10 minutes

Cook Time: 15 minutes

Serves 4

Ingredients

1 pound (16 ounces) boneless, skinless chicken breasts

1 teaspoon kosher salt

½ teaspoon ground black pepper

½ teaspoon garlic powder

½ teaspoon paprika

½ cup all-purpose flour

¼ cup oil, such as olive oil

Avocado Dip

1 avocado

1 lime

½ bunch cilantro

1 teaspoon salt

¼ teaspoon hot sauce

Tools

baking sheet

parchment paper

cutting board

chef's knife

measuring cups/spoons

bowl

blender

serving dish

Allergen Alert!

If you have a wheat allergy, replace the all-purpose flour with a wheat-free flour blend or coconut flour.

1. Preheat oven to 425°F. Line a baking sheet with parchment paper and set aside.

2. Carefully cut the chicken into 2-inch (5.1-centimeter) cubes.

3. Sprinkle the salt, pepper, garlic powder, and paprika over all sides of the chicken pieces.

4. In a bowl, roll the chicken in the flour until coated.

5. Place chicken on baking sheet, leaving 1 inch (2.5 cm) of space between each piece. Drizzle oil over the chicken.

6. Place the baking sheet in the oven for about 10 to 15 minutes or until chicken is golden on the outside and no longer pink on the inside.

7. While the chicken bakes, ask an adult to help you peel the avocado and remove its pit. Place the pulp in a blender.

8. Cut the lime in half and squeeze its juice into the blender.

9. Pull the tops of the cilantro from the stems and add to blender, along with the salt, pepper, and hot sauce.

10. Place the lid on the blender. Blend on high until smooth. If the mixture is too thick, add a tablespoon of water and blend again.

11. Pour the dip into a serving dish. Cover and place in refrigerator until served.

12. When the chicken is finished baking, allow to cool five minutes before serving with dipping sauce.

CORN DOG BITES
AND HONEY MUSTARD DIPPING SAUCE

There's no need to go to the fair to enjoy this summer favorite. Did you know you can make an egg-free corn coating for your hot dogs with flax and water? It's easy, and the result is a delicious and fun treat!

Prep Time: 20 minutes

Cook Time: 20 minutes

Serves 4

Ingredients

1 tablespoon ground flaxseed

3 tablespoons warm water

1 cup yellow cornmeal

1 cup all-purpose flour

2 teaspoons baking powder

1 teaspoon salt

1/3 cup pure honey

1/2 cup milk

1/4 cup oil, such as olive oil

4 hot dogs

Honey Mustard Sauce

1 cup coarse ground mustard

1/2 cup pure honey

1 teaspoon salt

Tools

standard muffin tin

12 muffin liners

2 small bowls

measuring cups/spoons

spoon

large mixing bowl

cutting board

chef's knife

toothpick

1. Preheat oven to 400°F. Line a muffin tin with paper liners and set aside.

2. Combine the flax and warm water together in a small bowl. Stir with a spoon to combine and then let sit for a few minutes.

3. In a large mixing bowl, combine the cornmeal, flour, baking powder, and salt. Mix well.

4. Add the flax mixture, honey, milk, and oil. Stir until combined.

5. Scoop the batter evenly into each muffin cup.

6. Cut each hot dog into three 2-inch (5.1-cm) sections and press a piece into each muffin cup.

7. Bake for about 20 minutes or until a toothpick comes out clean when inserted into the muffin.

8. Make the mustard dipping sauce while the muffins bake. Combine the mustard, honey, and salt in a small bowl and stir until mixed.

9. When the muffins are done, allow to cool for about five minutes before serving with the mustard dipping sauce on the side.

Allergen Alert!

Coconut flour or almond flour can replace the all-purpose flour to avoid wheat.

Be sure to read labels carefully on your hot dog packages. Soy, dairy, or wheat can be hidden in the ingredients list.

Soy milk or almond milk can be used to replace milk.

MINI MEATLOAVES

Meatloaf is a classic comfort food that is simple to make and yummy to eat. Applesauce makes these mini meatloaves fluffy, light, and absolutely delicious. You won't miss the eggs in this recipe!

Prep Time: 20 minutes

Cook Time: 30 minutes

Serves 4

Ingredients

1 small onion

1 ½ pounds (24 oz) lean ground beef or turkey

½ cup natural applesauce

1 tablespoon tomato paste

½ cup bread crumbs

1 teaspoon dried ground thyme

1 teaspoon salt

½ teaspoon ground black pepper

Sauce

½ cup ketchup

¼ cup yellow mustard

¼ cup packed dark brown sugar

Tools

baking sheet

parchment paper

cutting board

chef's knife

box grater

2 large bowls

measuring cups/spoons

scraper

Allergen Alert!

Looking to avoid wheat? Wheat-free bread crumbs can easily replace the traditional bread crumbs in this recipe.

1. Preheat oven to 375°F. Line a baking sheet with parchment paper. Set aside.

2. Carefully cut the onion in half, and then peel off the skin.

3. Place the box grater on the cutting board. Using the side of the grater with the large holes, gently grate the onion.

4. In a large bowl, combine the beef or turkey, applesauce, tomato paste, bread crumbs, thyme, salt, pepper, and grated onion.

5. Using clean hands, mix the meat until all of the ingredients are evenly combined.

6. Divide the meat into four equal pieces and form into loaf shapes on the baking sheet. Leave at least 2 inches (5.1 cm) of space between each mini loaf.

7. Place the ketchup, mustard, and brown sugar in a mixing bowl. Stir to combine.

8. Spread the sauce topping evenly over each loaf using a scraper. Then place the loaves in the oven.

9. Bake for about 30 minutes or until no longer pink inside.

10. Remove from the oven and allow to cool for five minutes before serving hot.

SPINACH-APPLE SALAD

Just like eggs, spinach is a great source of iron. You can create a nutritious and hearty salad with spinach. Get pumped up for this super salad topped with crisp apples and a sweet 'n tangy dressing!

Prep Time: 15 minutes

Cook Time: 10 minutes

Serves 4

Ingredients

Dressing

¼ cup apple cider vinegar

½ cup extra-virgin olive oil

¼ cup apple juice

2 tablespoons pure maple syrup

1 tablespoon Dijon mustard

¼ teaspoon salt

¼ teaspoon ground black pepper

Salad

2 Granny Smith apples

1 cup dried cranberries

¼ cup sunflower seeds

4 cups fresh spinach leaves

Tools

glass jar with lid

measuring cups/spoons

cutting board

chef's knife

mixing bowl

tongs

1. In a glass jar, combine the cider vinegar, olive oil, apple juice, maple syrup, Dijon mustard, salt, and pepper.

2. Screw lid on tightly and shake hard for about 30 seconds or until mixed well. Set aside.

3. Dice the apples into ½-inch (1.3-cm) pieces and place in a mixing bowl with the cranberries, sunflower seeds, and spinach.

4. Pour three-quarters of the dressing over the salad and toss gently with tongs.

5. Serve on plates with additional dressing on the side.

Allergens Eradicated!

No major food allergens found here!

POTATO PANCAKES

Are you a "brinner" person? That's right, go ahead and have breakfast for dinner! Pancakes can be made with lots of different foods, including potatoes. Crispy on the outside, fluffy on the inside, these delicious egg-free cakes are great for any meal!

Prep Time: 10 minutes

Cook Time: 5–10 minutes

Serves 4

Ingredients

2 medium Russet potatoes

¼ cup olive oil, divided

2 teaspoons salt

1 teaspoon ground black pepper

Tools

vegetable brush

vegetable peeler

cutting board

box grater

medium skillet

4-inch (10-cm) round metal
  biscuit cutter

small juice glass

spatula

tongs

Allergens Eradicated!

No major food allergens found here!

1. Scrub the potatoes clean and remove the skin using a vegetable peeler.

2. Place a box grater on a cutting board. Carefully grate the potatoes using the side with large round holes. Divide the grated potatoes into four equal piles and set aside.

3. Place a medium skillet over a burner set to medium heat. Place the biscuit cutter on the skillet and pour 1 tablespoon of olive oil inside the cutter.

4. Stuff one of the piles of grated potato inside the cutter. Use the bottom of the juice glass to pack it tightly. Sprinkle with ½ teaspoon salt and ¼ teaspoon pepper.

5. Carefully pull the cutter up and off of the skillet, leaving the potatoes on the skillet. Use the tongs to pull off the cutter if it is too hot to touch.

6. Allow to cook about three to five minutes, then gently turn over to cook the other side.

7. Remove the potatoes from skillet and place on a plate. Cover with foil to keep hot.

8. Repeat steps 3 through 7 for the remaining potatoes.

9. Serve hot as a side dish at breakfast or dinner.

CHEF'S TIP

Top your taters with your favorite condiments: ketchup, salsa, or even applesauce and cinnamon for a sweet treat!

MAPLE-GLAZED CARROTS

You know carrots are good for you, right? But how can you make them pop with flavor? These carmelized carrots will treat your taste buds to a sweet and scrumptious surprise! They are the perfect side to many dishes.

Prep Time: 10 minutes

Cook Time: 20 minutes

Serves 4

Ingredients

1 pound (16 oz) carrots

2 tablespoons oil, such as olive oil

1 teaspoon salt

2 tablespoons pure maple syrup

Tools

baking sheet

parchment paper

vegetable peeler

cutting board

chef's knife

measuring cups/spoons

Allergens Eradicated!

No major food allergens found here!

1. Preheat oven to 450°F. Line a baking sheet with parchment paper and set aside.

2. Peel the carrots with a vegetable peeler. Using a knife, cut the tops off each carrot. Then cut each carrot into 2-inch (5.1-cm) pieces.

3. Place carrots on baking sheet and drizzle with oil and salt.

4. Bake in oven for about 10 minutes or until carrots begin to brown.

5. Remove from oven and drizzle with maple syrup.

6. Increase oven temperature to 475°F. Bake an additional five to 10 minutes, or until the carrots have a deep brown color. Check after five minutes to avoid burning.

7. Serve immediately alongside your main course.

CHEF'S TIP

Sugar and spice make everything nice. Like a little spice? Sprinkle some cayenne pepper (about ¼ teaspoon) over the carrots during step 3.

STRAWBERRY ICE CREAM

Did you know you can combine just four ingredients to make ice cream? Eggs make ice cream rich, but you won't miss them in this sweet summer dessert that can be made or eaten any time of the year.

Prep Time: 10 minutes

Serves 4

Ingredients

1 pound (16 oz) frozen strawberries

1 tablespoon sugar

1 teaspoon almond extract

2 tablespoons coconut cream

Tools

food processor

measuring spoons

spatula

bowls, for serving

Allergen Alert!

If you are allergic to nuts, use vanilla extract in place of almond extract.

Coconut is classified as a fruit. But if you have a tree nut allergy, please talk to your doctor before eating it.

1. Place the frozen strawberries, sugar, and almond extract in a food processor and pulse it 10 times.

2. Turn the food processor on high until the mix looks as fluffy as soft-serve ice cream.

3. Scrape down the sides of the bowl with the spatula and pour in the coconut cream.

4. Pulse another 5 times and transfer to bowls for serving immediately.

5. Put leftovers in an airtight container in the freezer right away.

CHEF'S TIP

Substitute blueberries, raspberries, or blackberries for the strawberries if you prefer.

COCONUT VANILLA
PUDDING

Are you craving thick, delicious pudding but need to avoid eggs? Creamy and sweet, this delectable pudding can be made for your entire family or scooped into individual servings to take to school in your lunchbox.

Prep Time: 10 minutes

Cook Time: 4 hours (4 hours inactive)

Serves 4

Ingredients

2 cups coconut milk

½ cup sugar

3 tablespoons arrowroot powder

2 teaspoons vanilla extract

pinch of kosher salt

Tools

medium saucepan

measuring cups/spoons

whisk

mixing bowl

large bowl, for serving

Allergen Alert!

Coconut is classified as a fruit. But if you have a tree nut allergy, please talk to your doctor before eating it.

1. Place the coconut milk in a saucepan over medium heat. Bring to a simmer.

2. While the coconut milk heats, combine the remaining ingredients in a mixing bowl.

3. When the milk begins to simmer, slowly pour the sugar mixture into the saucepan, whisking while pouring to dissolve.

4. Continue to stir gently until the mixture begins to thicken.

5. Pour pudding into a serving bowl. Chill for at least four hours before serving.

6. Store leftovers in an airtight container in the refrigerator for up to one week.

CHEF'S TIP

Top the pudding with your favorite fruits or cookie crumbles for extra flavor!

LEMON CUPCAKES

Skipping cake because of the eggs? Think again! You can enjoy the cake you've been dreaming of, just without the eggs. Slightly sweet and tart to your tongue, these cupcakes are sure to please.

Prep Time: 15 minutes

Cook Time: 25 minutes

Serves 12

Ingredients

cooking spray

2 cups all-purpose flour

1 cup sugar

pinch of kosher salt

2 teaspoons baking powder

½ cup oil, such as grapeseed oil

1 cup milk (any kind)

2 lemons

Glaze

2 lemons

½ cup confectioner's sugar

Tools

standard muffin pan

2 mixing bowls

measuring spoons/cups

wooden spoon

box grater

cutting board

chef's knife

toothpick

small mixing bowl

fork

Allergen Alert!

Are you trying to avoid wheat?
Wheat-free flour blend can replace
the all-purpose flour in this recipe.

1. Preheat oven to 350°F. Lightly spray a muffin pan with cooking spray. Set aside.

2. Combine the flour, sugar, baking powder, salt, and baking powder in a large mixing bowl. Set aside.

3. Combine the oil and milk in a second bowl. Set aside.

4. Rinse the lemons. Carefully zest the outer yellow part of the rind using the side of the box grater with the small round holes. Add the zest to the oil and milk mixture.

5. Cut 2 lemons in half and squeeze the juice into the oil and milk mixture. Be careful to avoid seeds. Stir to combine.

6. Add the wet ingredients to the dry ingredients and mix well.

7. Fill each muffin cup two-thirds full. Bake for 20 to 25 minutes or until a toothpick inserted into the center comesout clean.

8. Make the glaze while the cupcakes bake. Cut 2 lemons in half and squeeze the juice into a mixing bowl.

9. Add the confectioner's sugar and mix with a fork until dissolved.

10. Remove the cupcakes from the oven and allow to cool completely. After the cupcakes have cooled, remove them from the pan and drizzle the glaze evenly over the tops.

11. Store leftovers in an airtight container for up to one week.

GLOSSARY

assemble—to put all the parts of something together

blend—to mix together, sometimes using a blender

consume—to eat or drink something

dissolve—to incorporate a solid food into a liquid by melting or stirring

drizzle—to let a substance fall in small drops

mash—to smash a soft food into a lumpy mixture

pit—the single central seed or stone of certain fruits

pulp—the soft juicy or fleshy part of a fruit or vegetable

simmer—to keep just below boiling when cooking or heating

slice—to cut into thin pieces with a knife

thaw—to bring frozen food to room temperature

whisk—to stir a mixture rapidly until it's smooth

zest—to scrape off the thin outer peel of a citrus fruit for use as flavoring

READ MORE

Clark, Pamela. *Allergy-free Cooking for Kids.* New York: Sterling Epicure, 2014.

Cook, Deanna. *Cooking Class: 57 Fun Recipies Kids Will Love to Make (and Eat!).* North Adams, MA: Storey Publishing, 2015.

McAneney, Caitie. *Peanut and Other Food Allergies.* Let's Talk About It. New York: PowerKids Press, 2015.

INTERNET SITES

Use FactHound to find Internet sites related to this book.
All of the sites on FactHound have been researched by our staff.

Here's all you do:
Visit *www.facthound.com*
Type in this code: 9781491480557